GRANDVIEW HEIGHTS PUBLIC LIBRARY
1685 WEST FIRST AVENUE
COLUMBUS OH 43212

Written and Illustrated by:
Téa Falemalama

Song:
Delta Rhythm Boys. "Dry Bones." Dry Bones, RCA Victor, 1952.

Skeletal Refrence:
"Dog Skeleton - 3D Model by Karab44." Sketchfab.com, 13 Oct. 2017. sketchfab.com/3d-models/dog-skeleton-cf24cbe2ada6472d968a60a40233e12d. Accessed 1 Nov. 2023.

Link to the website.
Check it out to explore more doggy anatomy!

Well, your toe bone connected to your

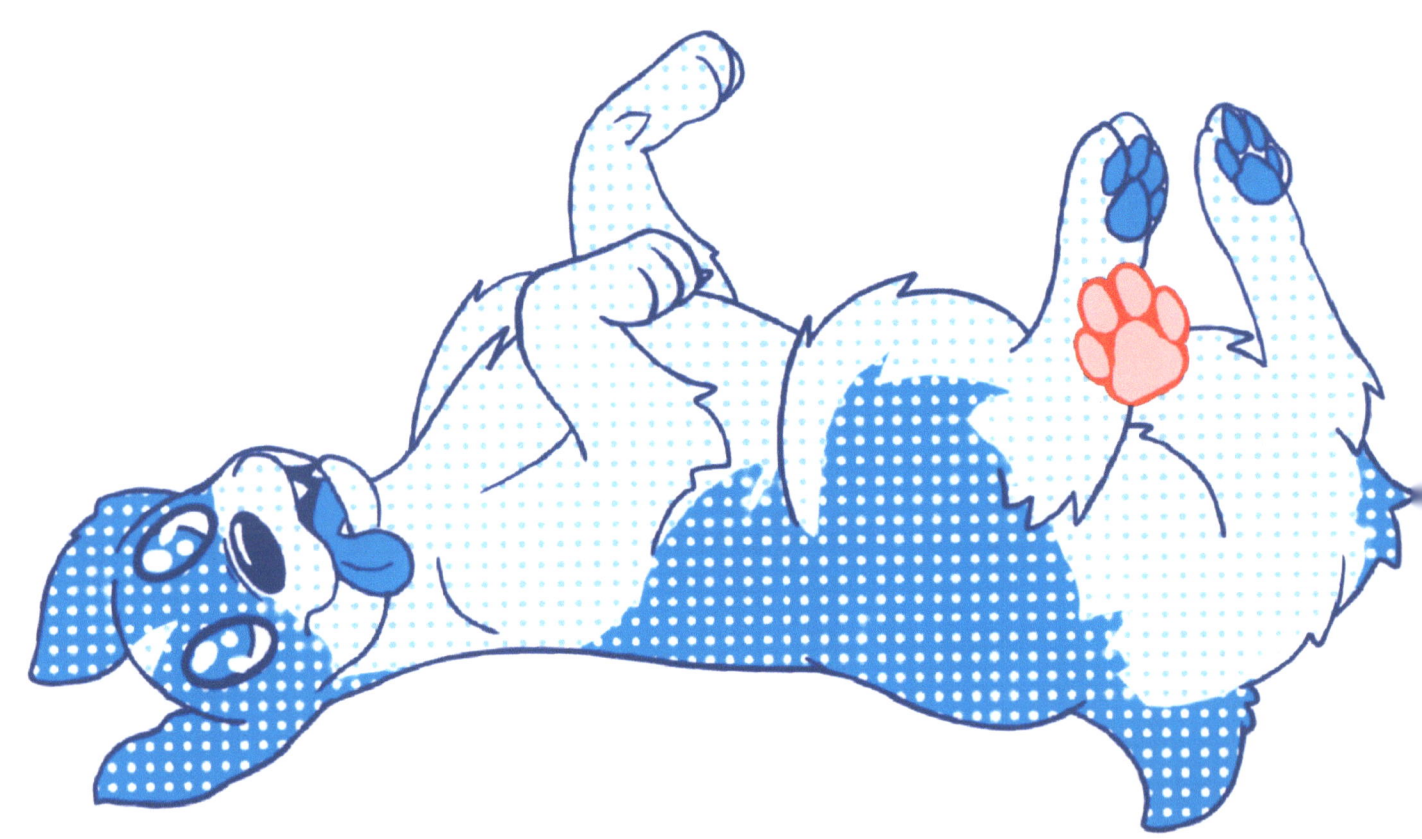

foot bone

PUPS SURE HAVE FANCY FOOTWORK! THEIR PAW IS HELD UP BY THE TOE BONES, AKA **PHALANGES**, WHICH SUPPORT THEIR WEIGHT AS THEY WALK. THE FOOT BONES, OR **METATARSUS**, DON'T TOUCH THE GROUND. INSTEAD, DOGS PRANCE ON THEIR TIPPY TOES!

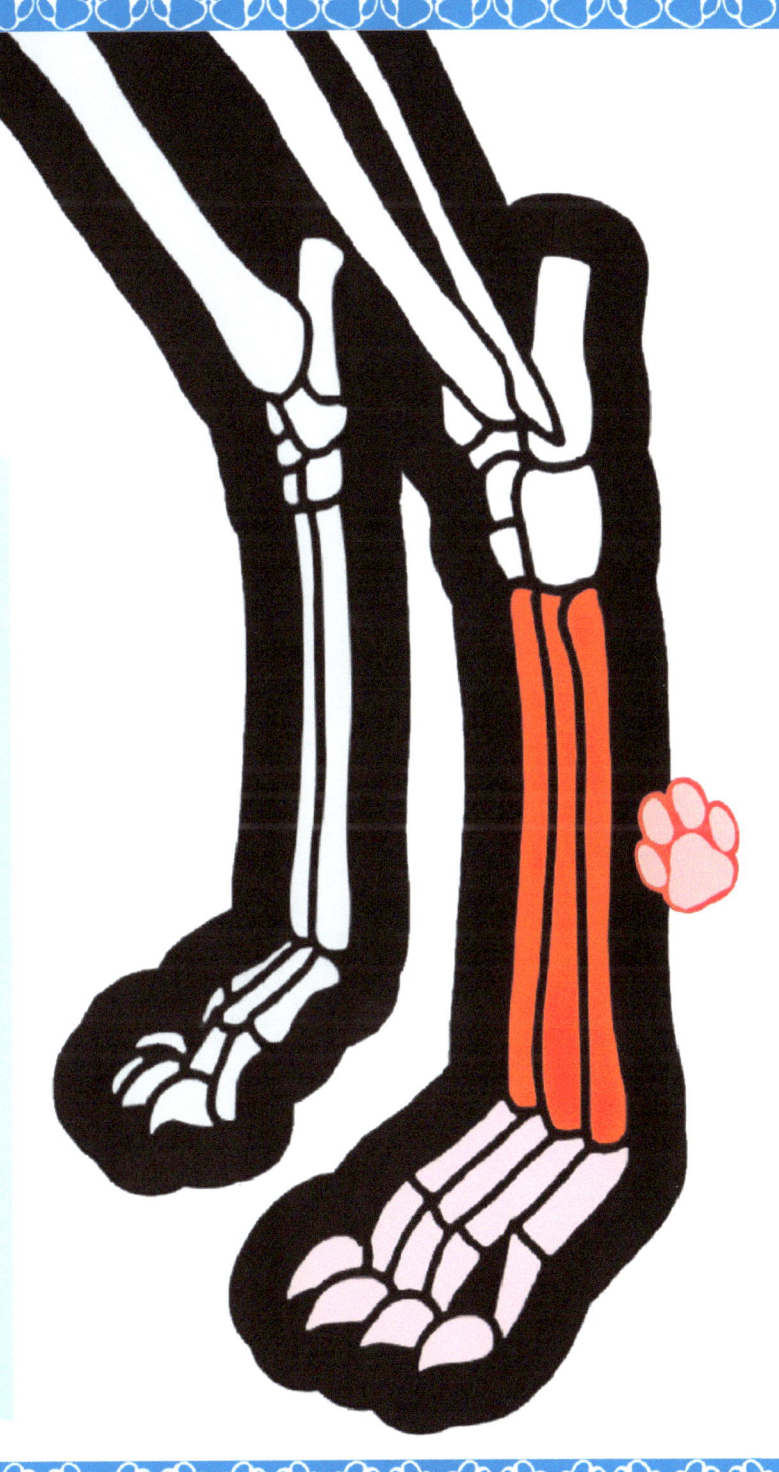

Your foot bone connected to your

ankle bone

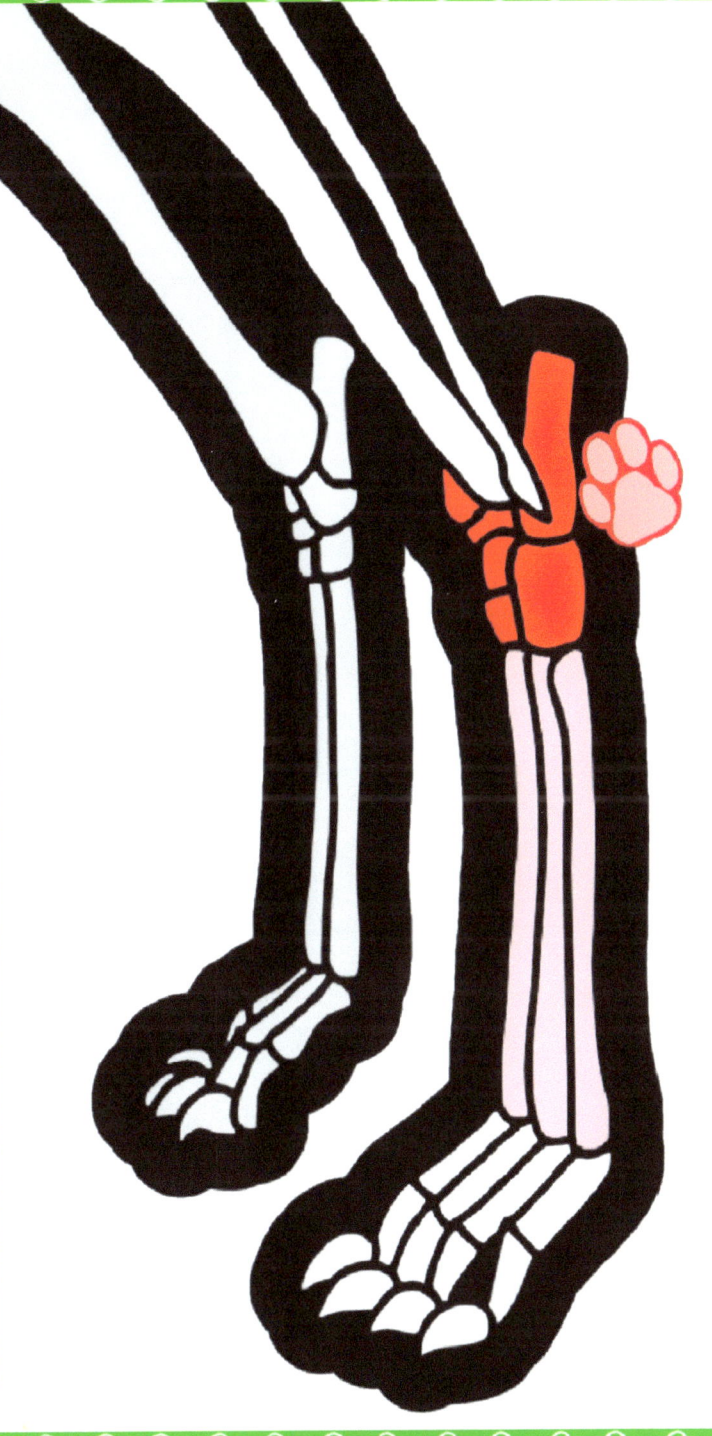

THIS GROUP OF BONES IS CALLED THE TARSAL BONES. THEY MAKE UP WHAT IN HUMANS IS THE ANKLE AND HEEL, BUT IN OUR FOUR-LEGGED FRIENDS, IS KNOWN AS THE HOCK.
STAND ON YOUR TOES AND SEE HOW YOUR HEEL POINTS UP TOO!

Your ankle bone connected to your

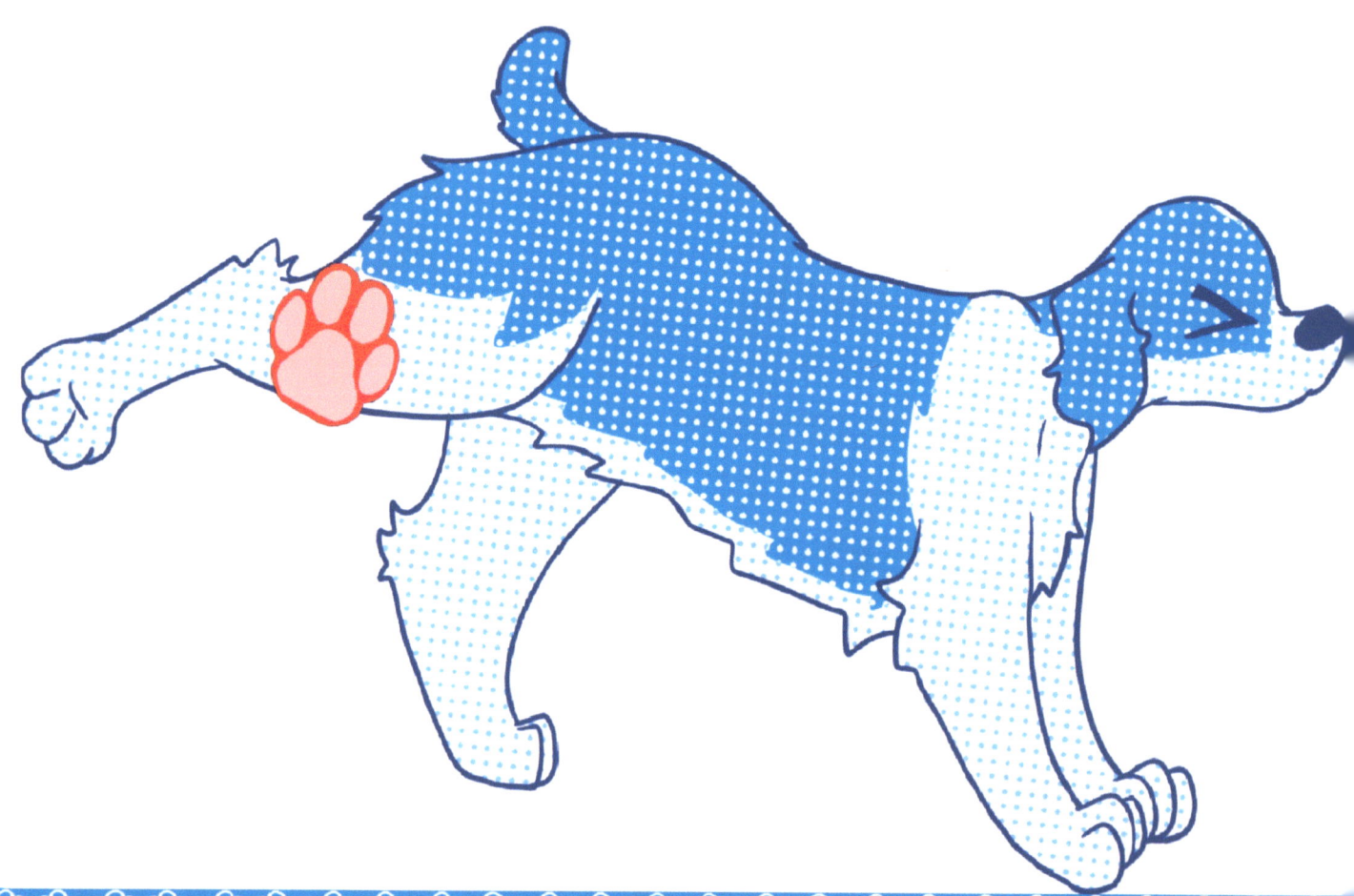

leg bone

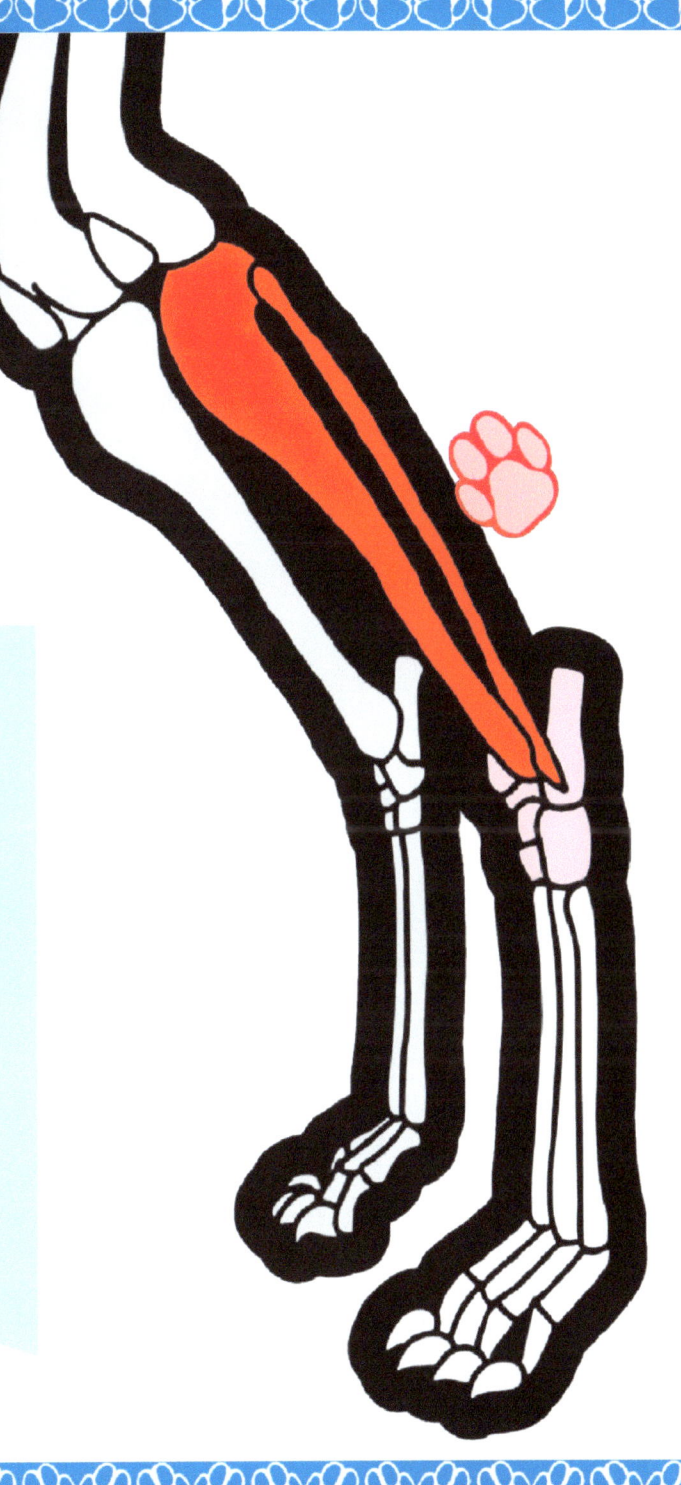

THE LEG BONE IS NOT ONE, BUT TWO BONES! THEY ARE CALLED THE FIBULA AND THE TIBIA. THE FIBULA IS THE SMALLEST OF THE TWO. THE FRONT LEGS ALSO HAVE TWO BONES IN THIS SECTION CALLED THE RADIUS AND THE ULNA.

Your leg bone connected to your

knee bone

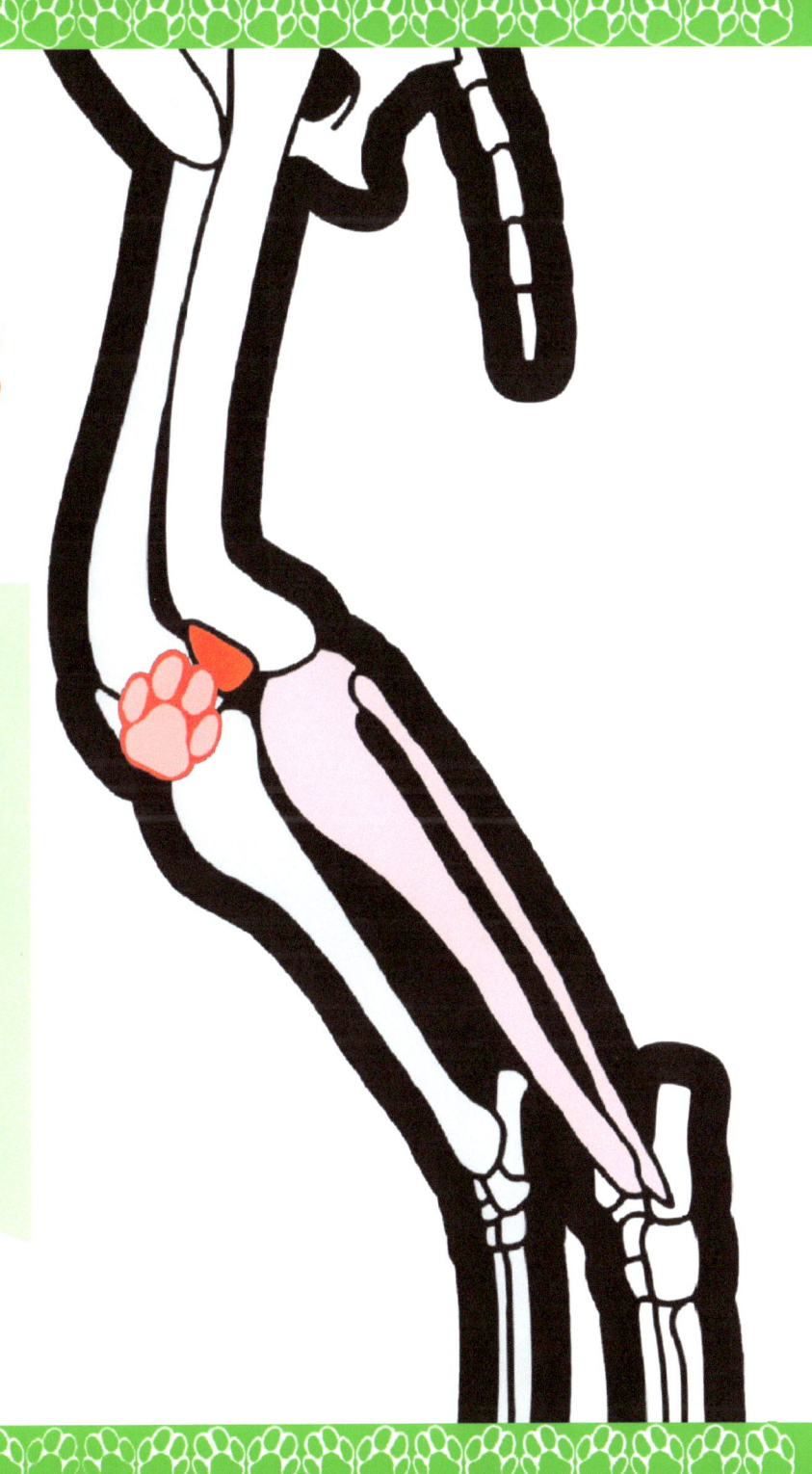

THE KNEE BONE, OR **PATELLA**, FORMS THE KNEECAP. IT IS CONNECTED TO STRETCHY TENDONS AND MUSCLES THAT HELP INCREASE THE MOTION OF THE LEG.

Your knee bone connected to your

thigh bone

THE THIGH BONE, OR **FEMUR**, WHILE NOT THE LONGEST, IS THE LARGEST AND STRONGEST BONE IN DOGS.

FUN FACT:
THE ULNA IS THE LONGEST BONE IN DOGS WHILE THE FEMUR IS THE LONGEST BONE IN HUMANS

Your thigh bone connected to your

hip bone

THE PELVIS OR HIP BONE IS VERY IMPORTANT. COMPOSED OF MANY SECTIONS OF STRONG BONE, IT HELPS PROTECT THE INTERNAL ORGANS.

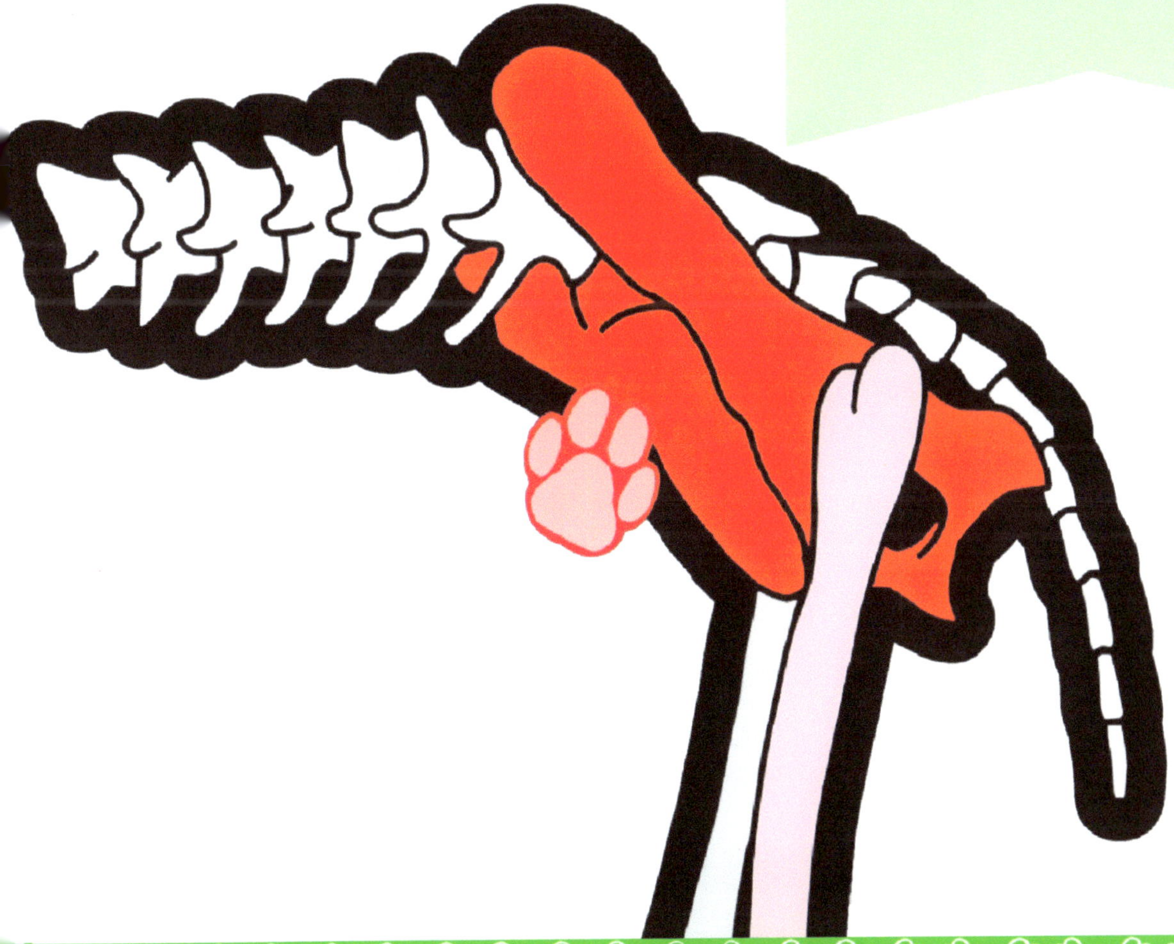

Your hip bone connected to your

back bone

THE BACKBONE, OR SPINE, HAS 5 SECTIONS:
- CERVICAL VERTEBRAE (7)
- THORACIC VERTEBRAE (13)
- LUMBAR VERTEBRAE (7)
- SACRAL VERTEBRAE (3)
- COCCYGEAL VERTEBRAE (DEPENDS ON THE LENGTH OF THE TAIL)

EACH BONE IN THE SPINE IS CALLED A VERTEBRAE

Count with me! Can you tell which section is which based on the number of vertebre?

Your back bone connected to your

shoulder bone

Count with me!
Can you tell which section is which based on the number of vertebre?

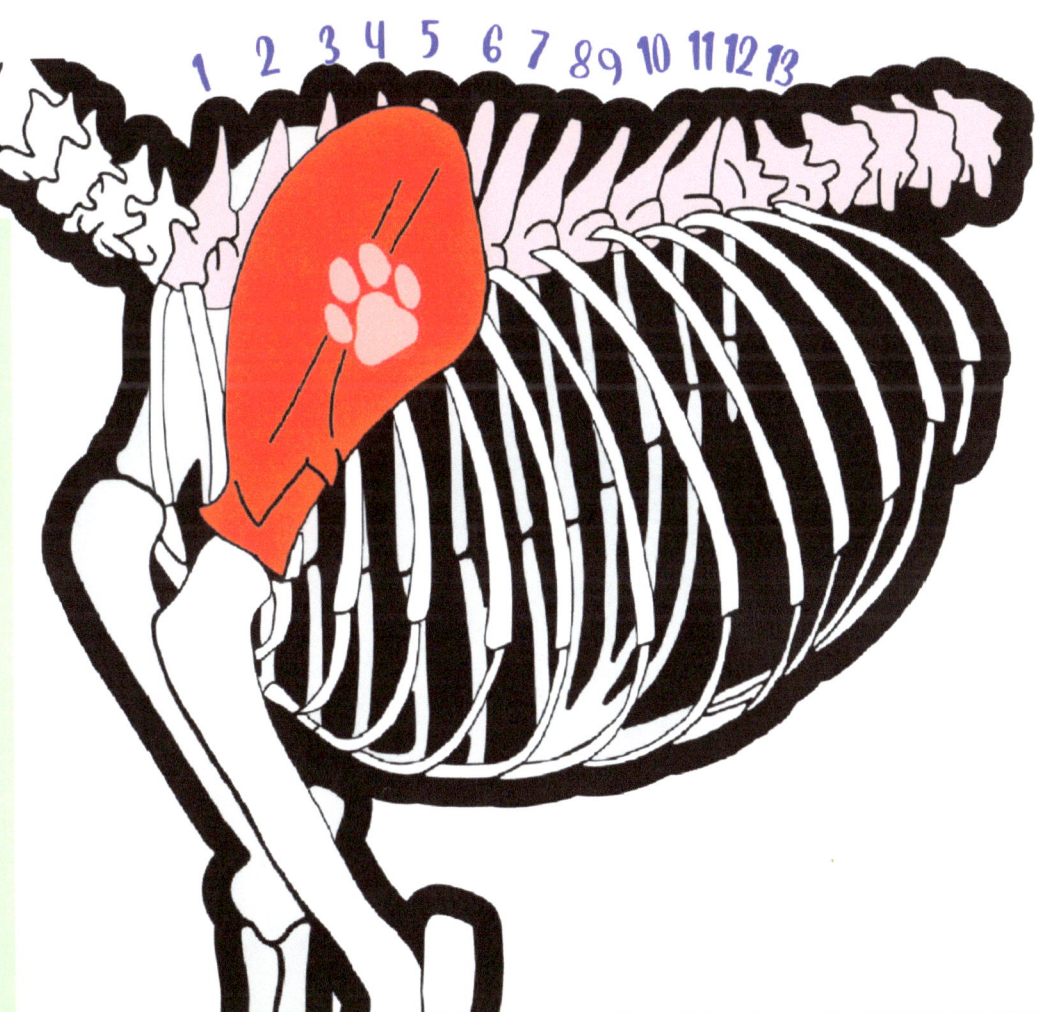

1 2 3 4 5 6 7 8 9 10 11 12 13

THE SHOULDER BONE, CALLED THE **SCAPULA**, IS LOCATED TO THE SIDE OF THE RIB CAGE IN DOGS, WHILE IT IS LOCATED ABOVE THE RIBS IN HUMANS.

Your shoulder bone connected to your

neck bone

THE NECKBONE IS ACTUALLY PART OF THE SPINE! IT IS THE SECTION ABOVE THE RIBS AND ALLOWS FOR FREE MOVEMENT OF THE HEAD.
DID YOU GUESS WHICH SECTION IT IS?

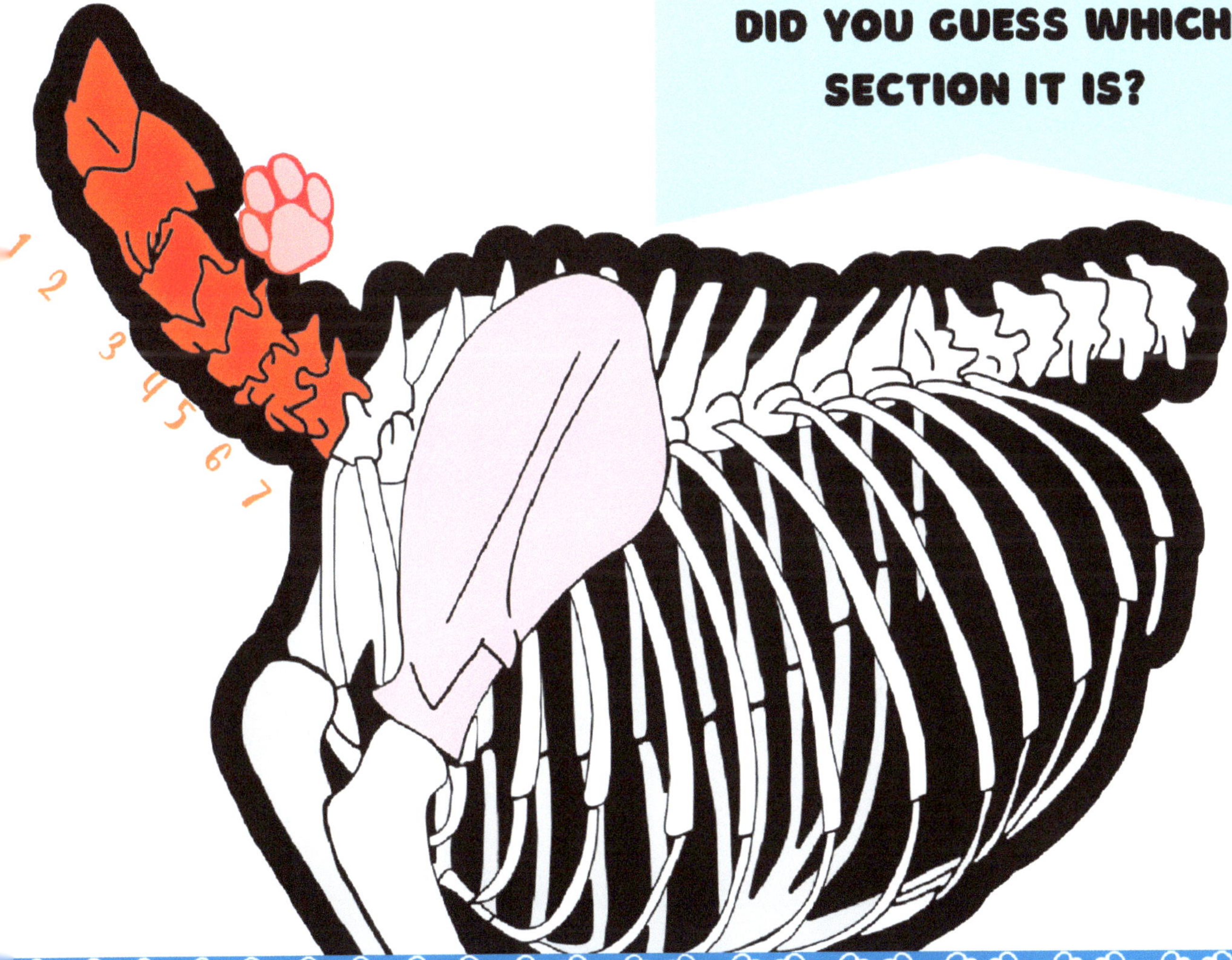

1 2 3 4 5 6 7

The neck bone connected to your

head bone

Last up is the head bone, aka the **SKULL**. This is the bone that houses the brain. It can come in many different shapes and sizes depending on what breed a dog is.

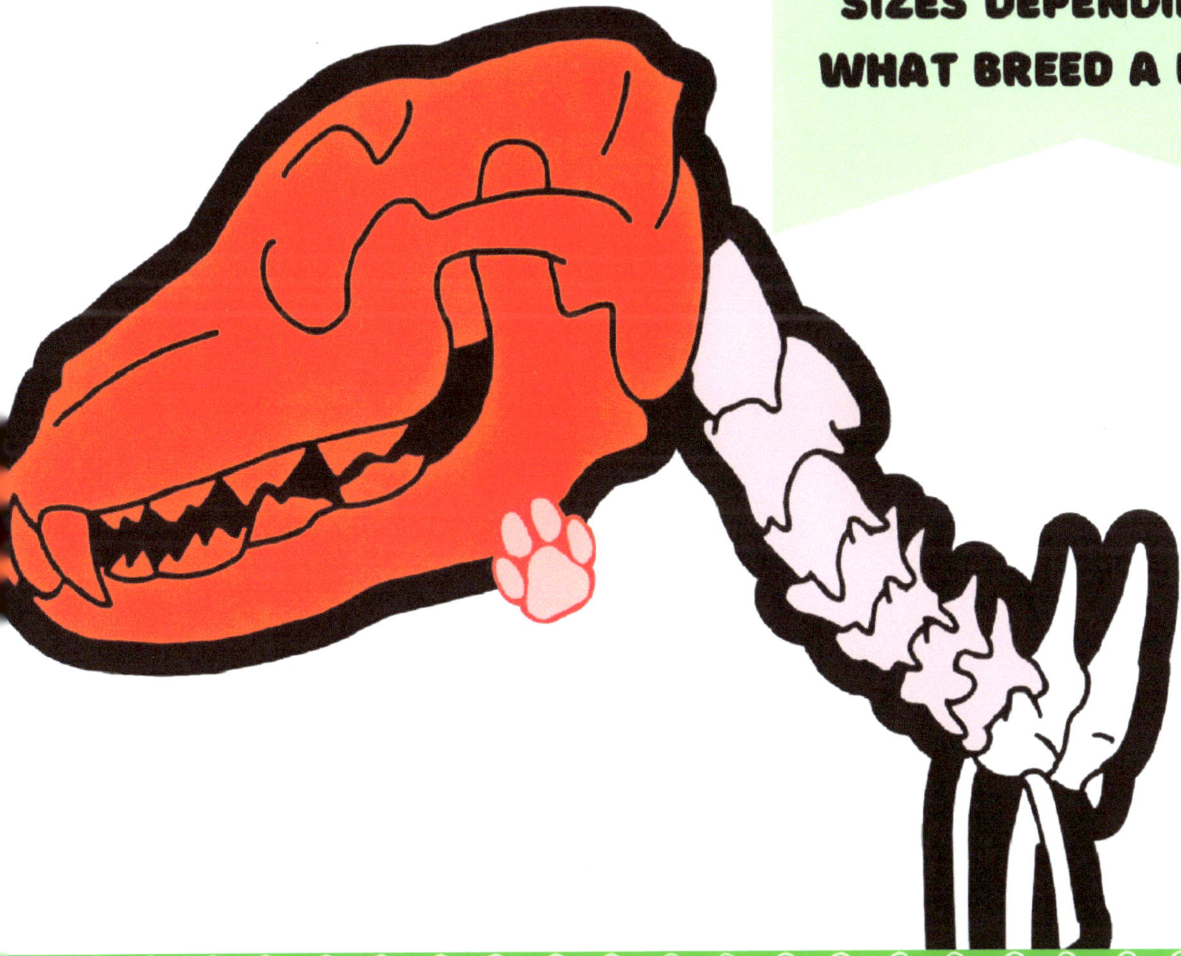

Count with me!

Answers:
cervical (7)
thoracic (13)
lumbar (7)
sacral (3)

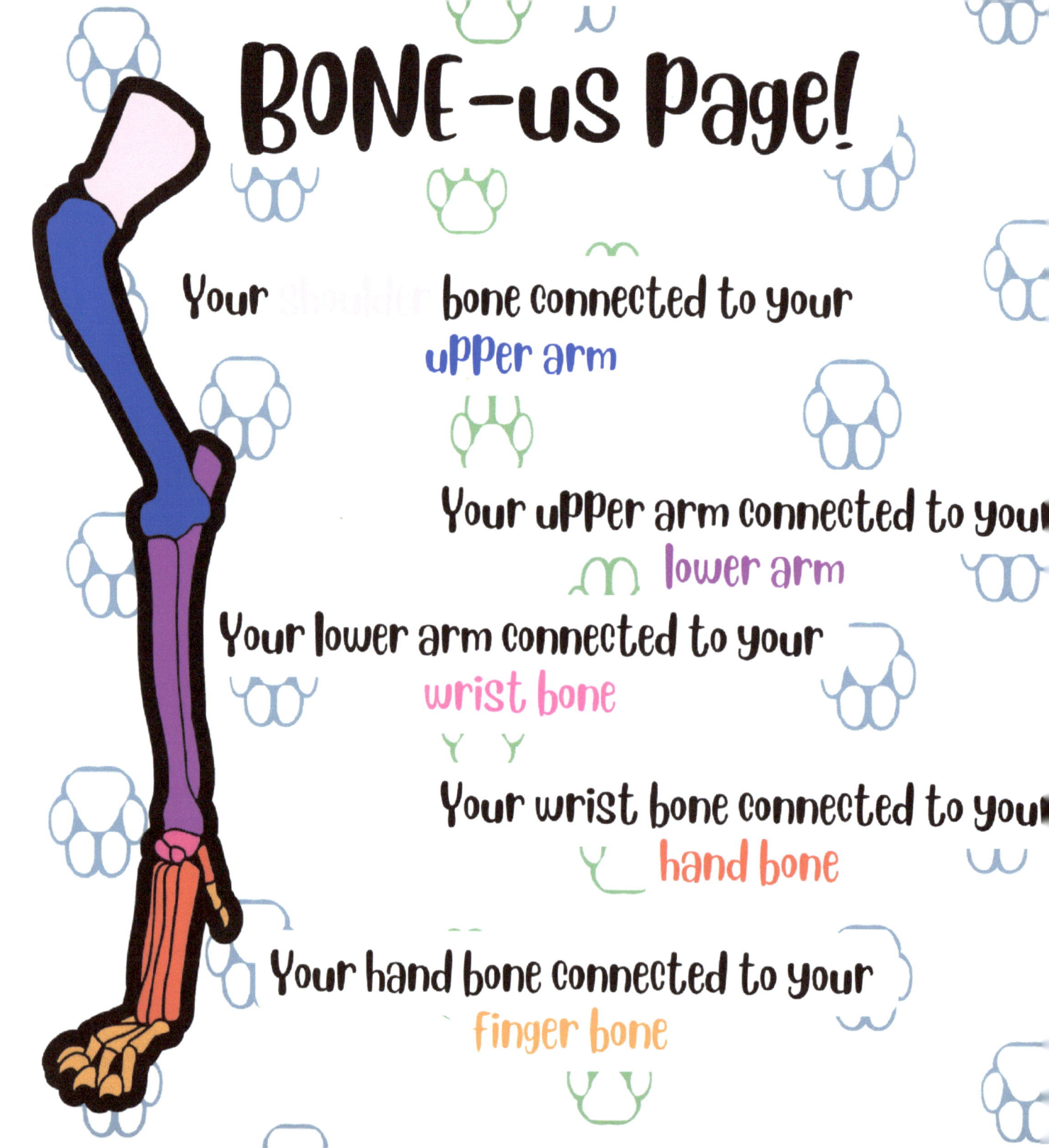

THE UPPER ARM, AKA THE **HUMERUS**, IS THE FIRST BONE OF THE FRONT LIMB OF A DOG.

JUST LIKE THE BACK, THE LOWER SECTION OF HIS LIMB HAS TWO BONES: THE **RADIUS** AND THE **ULNA**. DO YOU REMEMBER THE FUN FACT ABOUT THE ULNA?

THE WRIST IS MADE UP OF GROUP OF BONES CALLED THE **CARPAL BONES**. LIKE THE HOCK, IT ALLOWS FOR MORE MOVEMENT OF THE PAW.

THERE ARE 5 HAND BONES OR **METACARPALS**. LOOK HOW ONE IS HIGHER AND SHORTER THAN THE REST. THAT IS WHERE THE DEWCLAW IS LOCATED. THE SAME BONE AS YOUR THUMB!

IS THAT A THUMB I SEE? DOGS HAVE 5 FINGERS OR **PHALANGIES**. ALSO CALLED **DIGITS**. THEIR "THUMB" IS TOO HIGH TO TOUCH THE GROUND BUT CAN HELP WITH GRIP AND STABILITY.

Inspired by: Tucker

About the Illustrator

MY NAME IS TÉA FALEMALAMA. I WAS BORN AND RAISED IN NORTH CAROLINA AND ART HAS ALWAYS BEEN A PROMINENT PASSION OF MINE. I HAVE BEEN CREATING CHARACTERS AND STORIES FOR AS LONG AS I CAN REMEMBER. I MAJORED IN WILDLIFE BIOLOGY AT LEES MCRAE COLLEGE WHERE I SPENT MY TIME CARING FOR INJURED AND ORPHANED WILDLIFE AT THE WILDLIFE REHABILITATION CENTER ON CAMPUS. CREATING THIS BOOK WAS A UNIQUE WAY TO MERGE MY LOVE OF ANIMALS AND MY LOVE OF ART IN A WAY THAT CAN EDUCATE OTHERS IN A FUN WAY.

Printed in the USA
CPSIA information can be obtained
at www.ICGtesting.com
LVHW071118131024
793681LV00006B/37